THE
LITTLE WHITE LIES
GUIDE TO

MAKING
YOUR
OWN
MOVIE

Author's dedication: to Vincent

Published in 2017 by
Laurence King Publishing Ltd.
361–373 City Road
London EC1V 1LR
e-mail: enquiries@laurenceking.com
www.laurenceking.com

A catalogue record for this book is available
from the British Library.
ISBN: 978-1-78627-065-8

Art direction & design: TCO London
Illustrations: Studio MUTI

Printed in China

LITTLE WHITE LIES GUIDE TO

MAKING YOUR OWN MOVIE

IN 39 STEPS

MATT THRIFT

LAURENCE KING
PUBLISHING

06.   Intro

10.   Prep

Preparing to shoot your movie

12.   Breaking it down
15.   Storyboards
16.   Steal from the best
18.   The blueprint
21.   Watchlist #1 – The Greats
23.   Budget
24.   Embrace limitations
27.   Role call
29.   Watchlist #2 – Collaborators
30.   Places
32.   Rehearsal
34.   Kit
37.   Watchlist #3 – Innovators

39.   Shoot

Creating your movie

40.   Shapes
42.   Composition
45.   Faces
46.   Black & white
49.   Watchlist #4 – Monochrome magic
51.   Establishing
52.   Masters
54.   Two-shot
57.   Crossing the line
58.   Geography
60.   Movement
62.   Zoom
65.   Dolly & truck
67.   Watchlist #5 – Tracking shots
68.   Handheld
70.   Inside

73.	Outside
74.	Magic hour
77.	Night
78.	Driving
81.	On the lam
82.	Continuity
85.	Cutaways
86.	Recording dialogue
89.	Watchlist #6 – Sound
91.	Ambient sound

93. Post

Building and enhancing your story

95.	Organising
96.	Selecting material
99.	Watchlist #7 – Director's cuts
100.	Rhythm
103.	Watchlist #8 – Editing
104.	Music
107.	Finishing touches
108.	Finding an audience

111. Resources

112.	Budgeting
116.	Shooting schedule
120.	Equipment checklist
122.	Shot size table
124.	Planning your shots
126.	Storyboarding
131.	10 key resources

132. Index

136. Acknowledgements

The Little White Lies guide to making your own movie.

'**S**o you wanna be a picture maker,' said the man with the eyepatch to the scrawny teenager sitting across his desk. 'What do you know about?'

It was the early 1960s when a nervous, 15-year-old Steven Spielberg was ushered into the offices of the fearsome Hollywood legend, John Ford. Before the four-time winner of the Best Director Oscar, the cinematic titan responsible for the likes of *The Searchers*, *Stagecoach* and *The Grapes of Wrath,* piled into the room, dressed as a big-game hunter and with lipstick smeared across his face, the young man stood staring at the Frederic Remington paintings on the walls. The artist's work is characterised by lyrical, high-energy scenes of dust-parched landscapes featuring cowboys and Native Americans.

'Tell me what you see in that first painting,' growled Ford to the prying upstart.

Spielberg began to mumble something.

'No, no, no,' interrupted Ford. 'Where's the horizon? Can't you find the horizon? Don't point where it is. Look at the whole picture.'

Spielberg told the grizzled old master that the horizon was at the very bottom.

'Fine,' said Ford. 'When you can come to the conclusion that putting the horizon at the top of the frame or the bottom of the frame is a lot better than putting it in the middle of the frame, then you may someday make a good picture maker. Now get out of here.'

It's easy to think that a lot has changed when it comes to making movies since the days of Spielberg's apprenticeship, as recounted in Glenn Frankel's book *The Searchers: The Making of an American Legend* (2013). On a technical level, you'd be right. Filmmaking was an expensive business, a creative pursuit out of reach of anyone without access to serious funds and professional equipment. The advent of digital technology has changed all that. The physical means to make a film are now contained within the phone in your pocket.

What haven't changed over the last 50 – or even 100 – years are the basic rules of filmmaking. Cinema is a language, and, like any language, it has its own dialects, its own shortcuts, its own personal idiosyncrasies. What remain constant are the underlying grammatical rules that are all visible in the movies and TV shows we watch every day. This is a book about watching movies as much as it is about making them.

In his documentary *A Letter to Elia* (2010), a love letter to his cinematic hero Elia Kazan, Martin Scorsese talks about watching the James Dean film *East of Eden* (1955) over and over again: 'The more I saw the picture, the more I understood the presence of an artist behind the camera. Later I went back and tried to figure out how he did it, why it affected me so powerfully: the colour, the acting, the editing, the sound editing, camera movement, lighting. I studied them.'

These are just some of the elements that come together to create the cinematic illusion. Whether you're planning to pick up a camera and make a film, or simply want a better understanding of how the language of cinema works, nothing can take the place of watching as wide a spectrum of films as you can. Really watching them. Breaking them down into their constituent parts to discover how each works towards achieving a desired emotional or stylistic effect

I am a film lover who started writing about movies as a means to justify the hundreds and hundreds of films I watch year on year. The more I write about them, the greater my desire to understand how and why they affect me the way they do. I want to know what tricks the magicians had up their sleeves by looking for the subtle secrets they reveal on the screen.

It doesn't take long to begin noticing commonalities between even the most disparate stylists, the way different shots or camera movements, editing patterns or lighting effects can create certain moods. In many respects, it's about watching films differently, more objectively. A filmmaker doesn't want you to consciously think about what he or she is doing with the camera because it would take you out of the moment they're trying to create. Direction is really misdirection, but everything is there if you know where to look.

This isn't a technical manual, more an illustrated guide to gaining a better understanding of the means to achieve your cinematic goals. By breaking down the filmmaking process into its component parts, we can look at not just how to achieve a specific effect, but what it actually means and how to go about deploying it effectively. Don't just take my word for it, though; seek out the examples used to illustrate each chapter. Watch how the great masters of cinema construct a scene using the elements discussed here. Find your own examples, too. See how they compare, how they apply or can be adapted to suit the needs of your own scene.

What you use to shoot your film isn't important. What you choose to shoot and how you choose to shoot it is. Back in 2015 the American director Sean Baker found his film *Tangerine* the toast of the Sundance Film Festival. That raucous, micro-budget picture about a pair of transgender prostitutes was shot on the streets of Los Angeles entirely on an iPhone 5s with an anamorphic lens adaptor that cost less than $200. When the technical information appeared in the credits at the film's premiere, it elicited gasps from the audience and started an immediate bidding war.

In many respects, the hardest part of the filmmaking process occurs long before you decide to pick up the camera. Getting the creative juices flowing at the writing stage can feel like an uphill struggle that no amount of screenwriting guides can overcome. Keep things simple. Start filming something anyway. Shoot a scene, even if it's dialogue-free. Cut together some shots in different ways to see how the overall effect changes. Find inspiration through the act of filmmaking itself.

'I want to know what tricks the magicians had up their sleeves by looking for the subtle secrets they reveal on the screen.'

—

I hope that this guide will go some way towards illustrating how to put a film together, piece by piece. Don't expect the finished article to look like a pristine Hollywood blockbuster – there's a reason those films cost hundreds of millions of dollars to make. Yet it doesn't matter if you're John Ford or Martin Scorsese or if you got a GoPro for Christmas – the essential language of cinema remains constant, but also entirely malleable. Learn the rules before you break them. Now that basic equipment can be snapped up for negligible cost, there are no excuses not to digitise those cinematic dreams. If the 15-year-old Spielberg were walking out of that office today, you can bet he'd be out filming on his phone that very afternoon. He might not have ended up with *Jurassic Park*, but everyone has to start somewhere.

Prep

1. Breaking it down

'From now on, it will be total organisation.'
— TRAVIS BICKLE, *TAXI DRIVER*

It may sound like stating the obvious, but you can't underestimate the need for preparation when it comes to bringing a screenplay to life. Every single detail of your production must be thought through in advance. Grab a pen and a pad of paper. Pore over your script line by line, syllable by syllable, beat by beat.

The last thing you want is for a shoot day to grind to a halt while you search for a prop that happens to be an integral part of a scene. Poor preparation costs time, energy and money. It's likely that you'll encounter problems during the shoot that will demand improvisation, and these are problems best overcome if you know every detail of your production inside and out.

Scene by scene

- Think of your movie as a dish that you're about to cook. Make yourself a shopping list. Include every ingredient, from the location to the costumes to props and make-up. How many actors are in the scene? What props are they using? What time of day does the scene take place?

- Prepare a budget. Organise a shooting schedule, which is a timetable of all the shots you need to get and how long you have to get them. These will help to communicate your requirements to collaborators. They minimise the risk of problems.

- Every scene represents a series of problems that must be solved.

- The more you can solve in advance, the less you'll have to solve on the big day.

SHOPPING LIST
Will you choose complexity or simplicity?

2. Storyboards

To enter the more visual mindset of moviemaking, all you need is a pen, paper and a dash of imagination.

It's said that Alfred Hitchcock considered a film done and dusted once he'd completed his storyboard. Shooting the film itself was a mere technicality. While this may read like a tall tale, the reality is that Hitch rarely lunged for the viewfinder on set. He preferred to stage his shots well in advance of production. It's remarkable to see how closely a finished scene aligned with his initial conception.

The storyboard is a vital tool

- It forces you to think where you might place the camera for any given shot.
- It shows how those shots might later be cut together to produce a flowing scene.
- It's an effective means of communicating ideas to collaborators.

Film is a visual medium. It's often much simpler to sketch what you're aiming for than to attempt to describe the images you wish to capture.

You don't have to be a master illustrator to get your visual ideas down on paper. Many storyboards take the form of simple line drawings that show the camera angle and a sense of the frame in its most basic terms.

A storyboard is a rudimentary comic book that tells the story of your film in images. It's an opportunity to try out different ways of capturing a scene before arriving on set. It's a way of experimenting with and testing out ideas. You don't have to adhere to it on the day, but knowing the basic visual structure of a scene ensures no time is wasted when it comes to the shoot.

PICTURE PERFECT
Alfred Hitchcock –
one of cinema's most
assiduous storyboarders.

3. Steal from the best

'I steal from every single movie ever made. If my work has anything, it's that I'm taking this from this and that from that and mixing them together.' – QUENTIN TARANTINO

The great émigré filmmaker Billy Wilder had a sign mounted in his office that read: 'What Would Lubitsch Do?' It acted as a source of inspiration and a constant reminder of his hero, the brilliant director of early comedy Ernst Lubitsch.

As you're putting your storyboard together, it's a great idea to refer to how other filmmakers have tackled the questions you find yourself having to answer. Find out who your own hero is and take inspiration from them.

Look for inspiration in the unlikeliest places

There is an infinite number of ways that any scene can be shot and constructed. No single one of them is correct. It's not just the big moments for which you can turn to your cinematic idols for help. And don't just look to imitate or pay homage to their signature moves.

If you have what appears to be a straightforward conversation scene between two characters across a table, find as many examples as you can of a similar scene. Look for what makes them the same. Look for what makes them different.

FILMMAKER'S TIP:

Ask questions: is the scene shot over each character's shoulder, cutting between the two? When do the cuts arrive? Is the camera focused on the person talking, or the person listening? Is the whole scene captured in a single shot?

SOMETHING BORROWED ...
Take inspiration from master movie 'thief'
Quentin Tarantino.

4. The blueprint

'I could be just a writer very easily. I am not a writer. I am a screenwriter, which is half a filmmaker. But it is not an art form, because screenplays are not works of art. They are invitations to others to collaborate on a work of art.' — **PAUL SCHRADER**

The shooting script (which is a version of the screenplay used specifically for the shoot) is a production document. It is used by every member of the crew. It's where you should include all the details that have been worked out in pre-production. It forms the basis of a shooting schedule.

A screenplay must convey a number of elements:

- Narrative
- Character
- Dialogue
- Technical information

This is where storyboards become useful. Break down every scene into a series of shots. The shooting script must contain all the information required to get that shot filmed. If your screenplay is a mouth-watering description of a meal you're going to make, the shooting script is its recipe and list of ingredients. Assign every scene a number. Assign every shot within that scene a number too. →

KIND OF BLUEPRINT
Your screenplay contains a dog on a skateboard – but what other materials will you need to make that dream a reality?

This may all sound labour-intensive, but physically writing things down, making notes and developing a system will relieve much stress when it comes to the latter parts of the process. Numbering, documenting and organising should not preclude creativity. Having a clear image in your mind of the film you want to make will allow for more experimentation and flexibility when it comes to having fun in the edit.

Ensure that all requirements for every shot are included in your document – from wardrobe to location, from make-up to property. With all this in place, assess roughly how long each scene will take to film, as well as any financial and logistical requirements. How much will everything cost? How will everyone get to the shooting venue? Create a shooting schedule for each day's filming. Give yourself enough time to get the shots you need, but not so much that you're wasting the precious time of cast and crew who may be out there, freezing in a woodland glade.

FILMMAKER'S TIP:
Write a short description of each shot. Is it a close-up or a tracking shot? Any collaborators, from a full camera crew to an eager parent willing to hold a boom, will need to know the demands of a day's shooting in advance. You can also include a number that matches a shot to the relevant storyboard.

Watchlist #1

Our guide to essential deep research viewing.

1. Vertigo
ALFRED HITCHCOCK, 1958

This is a film that encapsulates its director's fixation with detail and the noxious power of on-screen beauty, as James Stewart enters into an obsessive affair with Kim Novak in this San Francisco-set chiller.

2. Citizen Kane
ORSON WELLES, 1941

This stellar debut movie about a publishing magnate brought down by ambition showcases a young master inventing neat new tricks with every magical scene. The unique form serves the material perfectly.

3. Man with a Movie Camera
DZIGA VERTOV, 1929

This evocative, experimental documentary depicts daily life in various Soviet cities, and stands as an early example of how movies don't have to tell conventional stories.

4. 2001: A Space Odyssey
STANLEY KUBRICK, 1968

The fruits of innovation and an exacting attention to detail are evident in every shot of Kubrick's astounding space opus, about intergalactic explorers who journey to the very cusp of human existence.

5. The Rules of the Game
JEAN RENOIR, 1939

Renoir's dazzling country-house satire showcases how to employ a large ensemble of actors. Lives intertwine and feed into a broad, trenchant statement on the stagnant state of France in the 1930s.

5. Budget

'All I need to make a comedy is a park, a policeman and a pretty girl.' — **CHARLIE CHAPLIN**

There's little getting away from the fact that making a film costs money, but how much money can vary wildly between projects. With a shooting script prepared, you can determine the film's budget. The cost of every aspect of production will need to be considered.

Resourcefulness is paramount

Recruit friends and family to fill out your cast and crew. The opportunity to participate in a production may well be payment enough. If you plan to pay one person for their services, whether as an actor or as a cinematographer, then you ought to work out a budget that sees everyone paid. Each person's services on your film are as valuable as the next. Equality is key.

You may have negotiated the out-of-hours use of a bar or restaurant – the promise of a little product placement when it comes to their business can go a long way. Your cast and crew, however, need more than that to survive. Feed your team throughout the day. Whatever else you can score for free, a food budget remains a priority.

For ultra-low-budget filmmaking, the chances of any return on investment remain slim, so keeping costs down is a necessity. But don't rule out the possibility of crowdfunding, whether online or among friends and family, to cover essential costs. Offer a small reward – maybe an invitation to a screening or a copy of the finished film.

FILMMAKER'S TIP:

With ample planning at the writing stage – and with a team already in place – costs can be brought down to next to nothing. Use what's at your disposal. If a location in your screenplay isn't available for free, rewrite the scene for somewhere that is.

CONSISTENT IS THE LIFE I LEAD
Mary Poppins's Mr. Banks
– a one-time paragon of
timing and efficiency.

6. Embrace limitations

'The enemy of art is the absence of limitations.'
— ORSON WELLES

No matter how nicely you ask, it's highly unlikely that NASA is going to launch a rocket as the dazzling backdrop to your hero's tearful farewell. Yet having to rethink the elements of a scene needn't be a compromise at all. Think about exactly what it is that is producing the climactic hit of emotion, and think of alternative ways in which to emulate it. Adjustments such as simplifying, streamlining and clarifying an idea may prove to be a major overhaul of an original concept. But with precise thought, they could lead to the discovery of new insights into a scene, a character or a theme that you hadn't previously considered.

When he wanted to shoot inside New York's Museum of Modern Art for his debut feature *Shadows* (1959), the director John Cassavetes was denied a permit on the grounds that he wouldn't be allowed to film the paintings. Instead, he rewrote the scene to take place in the museum's outdoor, public sculpture garden. It was a move that led to one of the film's best scenes, not least given the thematic link between the garden's masked figures and the masks worn metaphorically by the characters themselves.

Even the big guns aren't averse to a spot of last-minute improvisation to achieve the desired effect. With no money left and a scene that was missing a certain something, Steven Spielberg filled a neighbour's swimming pool with milk and a scuba-diving Richard Dreyfuss. The appearance of the fisherman's decapitated head wasn't in the shooting script, but it's one of the biggest jump scares in *Jaws*.

BLAST OFF
How do you achieve the effect of a space launch without the spaceship?

7. Role call

If there's one thing that we've learned from superhero movies, it's that there's nothing like a diverse, well-oiled unit of talented friends to save the day.

Film is often called a director's medium, but that doesn't mean you can make one on your own. You may choose to take on multiple roles, but it's useful to know what they might be and how important they are.

Who does what?

- **Cinematographer:** operates the camera. Lights the scene. Brings the shots in your head to life. Their focus is on the visuals, particularly in using their skill to emulate your vision of how the film should look and feel.

- **Production designer:** dresses the environment in which each scene takes place. Even on a micro-budget, a good production designer should be able to work magic with a bland space and ensure that you get the best out of the camera's capabilities.

- **Production manager:** organises the day-to-day running of your shoot. Manages everything from scheduling to personnel. When the production manager says it's time to move on, you move on.

- **Sound recordist:** don't underestimate the need to capture good sound. Find someone who knows what they're doing.

- **Make-up & wardrobe:** self-explanatory but vital. →

POWER UP
Assemble your own
unit of moviemaking
superheroes.

Bring in certain crew members ahead of others. Double up roles if necessary. A production manager can be a useful ally in sharing much of the organisational and administrative workload, while finding yourself a talented cinematographer would be beneficial during the storyboarding phase of your project.

If you have a smartphone in your pocket and want to go out and produce something on your own, that's absolutely fine. But bringing in collaborators can lend your production a sense of purpose. Ideas can be discussed and developed, problems can be solved. If you haven't managed to consolidate your concept, talk it through with your friends, and you might even discover something new.

FILMMAKER'S TIP:

Take your time bringing together the group of people you want to work with. It's important that everyone is on the same page. These are people you'll be spending long, stressful hours with. There will be arguments. There might be tears. A cohesive, fired-up unit can make all the difference.

Watchlist #2

Celebrating the key players on great movie productions.

1. Cinematographer: Days of Heaven
TERRENCE MALICK, 1978
This tragic fairytale about crop harvesters in the Texas Panhandle is lifted to the realms of greatness by its extraordinary, quietly radical cinematography, care of Néstor Almendros and Haskell Wexler.
Watch this and learn how to shoot at night.

2. Production designer: The Royal Tenenbaums
WES ANDERSON, 2001
David Wasco was the production designer charged with bringing Wes Anderson's candy-coloured daydreams to life for his sublime saga on the death and gradual rebirth of a family of cracked geniuses.

3. Producer: Pulp Fiction
QUENTIN TARANTINO, 1994
One of the tightest producer-director relationships in Hollywood is that between Quentin Tarantino and Harvey Weinstein. A respected and feared titan of the industry, Weinstein is a protector (and occasional alterer) of the artist's vision.

4. Sound recordist: A Wedding
ROBERT ALTMAN, 1978
This ensemble comedy is a head-spinning logistical feat, employing the director's customary tactic of mic'ing up lots of actors at the same time and creating a glorious, multilayered cacophony of voices.

5. Make-up: Dr. Jekyll and Mr. Hyde
ROUBEN MAMOULIEN, 1931
An extremely effective use of make-up can be seen in this chiller from ex-theatre director Mamoulien, as he and his team transform leading man Fredric March from kindly Victorian-era doctor to depraved prowler.

8. Places

*'Choosing location is integral to the film: in essence,
another character.'* — **RIDLEY SCOTT**

Places and spaces captured on film can say a lot about the world. How
these locations are used can often express more about who these
characters are in a single shot than entire pages of dialogue.

How a space is shot can be as important as selecting the space
itself. How do characters interact with and inhabit their immediate
surroundings? Where do they work, sleep, eat, drink?

Those with personal fortunes aside, few can afford the luxury of
a custom-built set, so work with what is available. Think of the free
tools at your disposal. How do night and day affect a space? How does
the weather affect the mood of a scene? How do busy streets or isolated
expanses reveal a character's state of mind?

Spot the difference

The British director Mike Leigh has shot a number of films on the
streets of London. Yet the city as seen in his film *Naked* (1993) is a
very different beast from that in *Happy-Go-Lucky* (2008). The latter
finds sunny days and bright colours a match for the eternal optimism
of its protagonist; the former captures a dangerous nocturnal world as
a desolate study in alienation and loneliness.

RUNNING HOT AND COLD
Top: the sun of *The
Sound of Music*. Bottom:
the snow of *Everest*.

9. Rehearsal

'One of the most helpful things the director can do is invite the actor to improvise scenes that do not appear in the script but that in narrative terms have taken place just before the scene that is being presently explored.'
— ALEXANDER MACKENDRICK

Rehearsal is an invaluable part of your pre-production process. It's an opportunity for cast members to find their way into the material, and a chance to refine a screenplay. Hearing dialogue spoken out loud by other people – and not the voices in your head – can swiftly bring any problems into focus.

Start with a read-through of the script with the entire cast. Begin discussions on aspects of character, either individually or as a group. Break dialogue down into 'beats' – which are like important moments that create the intended rhythm of the film – as a way of setting the tone and pace of a scene.

Permit actors to offer as much input as possible, both in terms of character and staging. It's a collaborative process, all the more so at this stage. Allow cast members to bring their own interpretations to the table before giving specific notes on performance.

Guide the cast through the script scene by scene. Get everyone on their feet. Rehearsal provides an opportunity for you to work out aspects of rudimentary staging, even if you don't have the privilege of rehearsing in the space where you'll be shooting.

FILMMAKER'S TIP:
- Record the rehearsal process on your phone.
- Test out shot ideas while working with the cast.
- There's no wrong way to do something, until you've found the right way.

PLAYDATE
Rehearsals must be organised, but they can also be great fun.

10. Kit

'Pick up a camera. Shoot something. No matter how small. No matter how cheesy. No matter whether your friends and your sister star in it. Put your name on it as director. Everything after that you're just negotiating your budget and fee.' — JAMES CAMERON

The technology needed to make a movie is now accessible to anyone. A smartphone offers immense visual recording power that fits right in the pocket.

Small is beautiful

Sean Baker's film *Tangerine* (2015), about a pair of transsexual hustlers making their way across Los Angeles on foot, was shot entirely on an iPhone. Monte Hellman's *Road to Nowhere* (2010), was shot on a Canon 5D. Lars von Trier's meta musical *Dancer in the Dark*, from way back in 2000, was filmed on a consumer-grade Sony DV cam. If you want to shoot on a camcorder, a friend probably has one. Be nice to them. →

CLASSIC COMBO
Pick the right tools for the job at hand, and innovate if necessary.

The sheen of professionalism no longer equates to a massive financial outlay for equipment. When it comes to additional paraphernalia – the equipment you need to keep your camera steady or make it move – tripods can be had for a pittance online. And you don't necessarily need to lay tracks to be able to push the camera towards a subject (a 'push-in', to use the technical term): a tripod fixed to a kid's scooter or shopping trolley can work a treat.

Invest in a decent microphone, and keep sound recording separate from your image recording. The mics on smartphones and HD cams are generally inferior to a proper, standalone mic.

Embrace your limitations

Accept that your film isn't going to look like a $150 million Hollywood blockbuster shot on 70mm film. But don't think of your camera's technical specifications as limitations.

FILMMAKER'S TIP:
- Get good sound.
- Get great performances.
- Tell your story.
- Tell it with imagination.

CAMERA OBSCURA
A compact mini DV cam is a level up from your smartphone.

Watchlist #3

The true radicals of cinema got the best from modest means.

1. Shadows
JOHN CASSAVETES, 1959

Perhaps the ultimate example of on-the-lam DIY filmmaking, Cassavetes' lyrical film depicts the love lives of jazz musicians in a way that channels the searching, intuitive and musical properties of the jazz form.

2. Frances Ha
NOAH BAUMBACH, 2012

The snappy, 'just do it' spirit of the great indie innovators is alive and well in Noah Baumbach and Greta Gerwig's comic tale of a city girl trapped in twentysomething economic purgatory.

3. The Evil Dead
SAM RAIMI, 1981

This extraordinary homemade horror classic saw its makers raid the larder to produce buckets of fake blood and then later attach a movie camera to the front of a dirtbike to emulate a vengeful woodland spirit.

4. Primer
SHANE CARRUTH, 2004

No one said time travel had to be simple, but in Shane Carruth's micro-budget brain teaser, the director unravels the mysteries of the time–space continuum with the help of two guys, a garage and a big metal box.

5. Following
CHRISTOPHER NOLAN, 1998

Before money became no object for the director of The Dark Knight *and* Interstellar, *he made this London-set tale of voyeurism with a bunch of mates, a 16mm camera and available light, all during his spare time over evenings and weekends.*

Shoot

11. Shapes

'I usually do suggest one format over another for a particular film but the final decision belongs with the director, as with any other aspect of production. Like most of the decisions I make it is, for the most part, an instinctive one based on a sense of the film I get from reading the script.'— ROGER DEAKINS

Movies come in all shapes and sizes. Even the most basic digital camera offers a variety of framing options, known as the aspect ratio and written as two numbers separated by a colon. The first number is a unit of width, the second a unit of height. Do you want the picture to be closer to a square (4:3, 1:85) or a rectangle (16:9, 2.35:1)?

The more rectangular widescreen frame became popular from the mid 1950s, as exteriors and action sequences took on a greater sense of scale. The squarer 4:3 format used since cinema's early days began to die out as films expanded their scope and moved away from dialogue-driven interiors. The movie *Bonnie and Clyde* (1967) was shot in 1:85, giving it a playful, almost vintage feel.

Both David Lean and Quentin Tarantino chose the super-wide aspect ratio for their respective films, the romantic epic *Ryan's Daughter* (1970) and the verbose chamber western, *The Hateful Eight* (2015). Lean employed his massive picture as a way to dwarf his characters against the Irish landscape, while Tarantino's film largely takes place inside a boarding lodge. A shorter frame can build a feeling of intimacy. It can also create a claustrophobic sense of your subject being boxed in by the world.

> **FILMMAKER'S TIP:**
> If there are two characters talking in widescreen, take into account what to do with the added space surrounding them. How does it change the feeling of the scene? How can compositions be adjusted and enhanced?

VISTA VISION
Top: *Bonnie and Clyde.*
Centre: *The Hateful Eight.*
Bottom: *Ryan's Daughter.*

12. Composition

'Cinema is a matter of what's in the frame and what's out.' — **MARTIN SCORSESE**

Everything within a frame means something. Every element derives meaning from every other element. This harmony is what's known as mise en scène. There are basic rules to composition that are there to be either followed or broken. Is it best to frame a character or object in the centre, or use the rule of thirds (breaking the frame up into three equal horizontal segments)?

Every approach says something different. What can you reveal about a character with any and every shot? Is the task to empower this person, for example, to make them appear larger than life? If that is the case, shoot them from below their eye-line.

Alienation vs. unity

Italian filmmaker Michelangelo Antonioni was a master at expressing the relationship between people and spaces. *L'Avventura* (1960) and *Red Desert* (1964) depict people inhabiting a place while wholly disconnected from both the environment and one another. Stories are told through the way figures are positioned within the frame.

In complete contrast, look at the piano scene from Howard Hawks's film *Only Angels Have Wings* (1939). Many of his films use the cohesion of a group as a major theme, and these sequences show how he brings each individual into the frame, united in a single purpose. The very composition of the shot – where people are placed and where their attention is drawn – evokes a togetherness that is at odds with Antonioni's sense of the distance between people.

FILMMAKER'S TIP:

Ask questions about the relationship between the characters and the space they inhabit. Is it overwhelming them? Engulfing them? Or are they filling it with their physicality or personality?

FULL HOUSE?
Top: *Red Desert*.
Bottom: *Only Angels Have Wings*.

13. Faces

'Leone believed, as Fellini did, as a lot of Italian directors do, that the face means everything. You'd rather have a great face than a great actor in a lot of cases.'
— **CLINT EASTWOOD**

A close-up of the human face is a powerful weapon. It's a psychological magnifying glass in which the smallest change in expression carries a seismic force. It's an invitation to close scrutiny. A way of highlighting what would be imperceptible at any greater distance. It's a means of homing in on subtle emotional shifts. A means of building intimacy or tension.

John Cassavetes, the godfather of American independent cinema, used a series of punishing close-ups in his appropriately titled film *Faces* (1968). There's a voyeuristic quality to the way in which he invades the personal space of his actors with his tight compositions. Fraught, drunken battles between characters take on the quality of raw confession. While Cassavetes would use the close-up as a means of studying behaviour, Sergio Leone would mine its possibilities for ratcheting up tension.

The final set piece of Leone's epic *The Good, the Bad and the Ugly* (1966) is a masterclass in how different distances between camera and subject can be cut together to enhance a sense of expectation. Three men – Clint Eastwood, Lee Van Cleef and Eli Wallach – are in a Mexican stand-off, all breathlessly waiting for each other's reaction, trigger fingers itching. Leone moves through a series of varying close-ups, moving closer and closer until the screen is filled with just pairs of eyes. The compositions are inseparable from the increasing speed with which Leone cuts between them. Microscopic movements take on an operatic sense of scale. The audience holds its breath. Then Clint draws ...

A FACE IN THE CROWD
Top: *Faces*. Centre: *The Good, the Bad and the Ugly*. Bottom: *The Seven Year Itch*.

14. Black & white

'I believe that the black-and-white photograph, or rather the grey zones in the black-and-white photograph, stand for this territory that is located between death and life.'
— **W.G. SEBALD**

There's little escaping the timeless, romantic nature of black-and-white cinematography and the vivid memories of old movies. Think of Martin Scorsese's down-and-out boxing saga *Raging Bull* (1980) or, more recently, Noah Baumbach's twinkling rite-of-passage comedy *Frances Ha* (2012). When Woody Allen decided to shoot his masterpiece *Manhattan* (1979) in black and white, he said it was because it was the way he remembered the New York of his childhood. Shooting in monochrome was, not so long ago, considered a commercial death sentence in Hollywood, allied to the belief that cinema audiences wanted their screen dreams to offer them bursts of bright colour as an antidote to the stress of their mundane working lives. Then, in 2012, a film called *The Artist*, by the French director Michel Hazanavicius, picked up the Best Picture Oscar, proving that if the vehicle is good enough, audiences are happy to alter their viewing habits.

Monochrome nostalgia

Choosing to shoot in black and white is certainly a statement. Be sure that the decision is determined by the material – there is a natural nostalgic baggage that comes with the use of monochrome. Shoot in colour, and add the black and white later as a special effect. Although it's easy to film with a black-and-white filter on a smartphone, post-conversion means that both options are available. →

PAINT IT BLACK (AND WHITE)
If you want to make it monochrome, know why you're doing it.

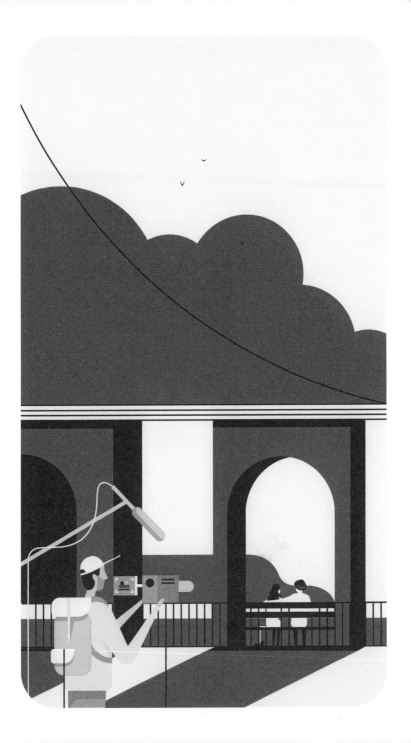

With high contrast levels (where the whites are very light and the blacks very dark), it's possible to create the kind of dramatic effects with lighting that would be less pronounced in a colour film. It can heighten atmosphere, emphasising the overall mood of a piece.

See the world in a different way

Try removing colour from your film – it allows the viewer to see the world in a different way. Shooting in black and white also draws attention to composition and form. It carries a rawness that might reflect the lives of the characters being filmed. It's another card to play: no better or worse than shooting in colour, just an alternative means of expressing feeling and ambience, and realising the world of your film.

FILMMAKER'S TIP:

If you've decided on using black and white, it's worthwhile shooting some test scenes before your main shoot to see the effect of different contrast levels. Does this mode affect things like how costumes look, how much light is needed or sequences filmed at night?

Watchlist #4

Five films that showcase the beauty of monochrome visuals.

1. Schindler's List
STEVEN SPIELBERG, 1993

At the same time as making multiplex-bound CG marvel Jurassic Park, Spielberg encapsulated the unalloyed starkness and brutality of the Holocaust by filming Schindler's List in cold black-and-white tones.

2. Raging Bull
MARTIN SCORSESE, 1980

This impressionistic biography of middleweight contender Jake LaMotta is designed to look like a tale from a bygone era, its high-contrast monochrome aesthetic burning like a flashbulb in the eye.

3. La Haine
MATHIEU KASSOVITZ, 1995

Black and white is occasionally used by filmmakers as a signpost for nostalgia. Not so with Mathieu Kassovitz's virulently angry hymn to marginalised Parisians, fighting for their lives in warzone-like banlieues.

4. Eraserhead
DAVID LYNCH, 1977

Lynch's stellar debut feature is as unassailably weird today as it was back in 1977, telling the surreal tale of a nervy loner saddled with some alien childcare. The black-and-white visual texture looks as though the celluloid has been rubbed over with sandpaper.

5. The Artist
MICHEL HAZANAVICIUS, 2011

This awards-hauling salute to cinema's earliest days emulates the warm visual glow of the silent era. The tale of a lovelorn matinee idol was shot in full colour and altered in post-production.

15. Establishing

An establishing shot – generally the first shot of a scene or even a movie – gives the viewer a sense of geography. It's a location signpost. It serves as an introduction to a scene, or a brief interlude before the main action occurs. It can give your film context.

Think carefully about whether an establishing shot is needed at all. One that contains no character or narrative information can easily be superfluous if it focuses on location or setting. Yet establishing shots have the potential to be poetic. They can be filled with valuable meaning. The location of your film can become a character in and of itself. It can create the sense of a breath taken between the beats of a story.

Take Andrew Haigh's *45 Years* (2015) as an example. The film is divided into the days of the week leading up to a fateful wedding anniversary. Each day is separated by a wide shot of Charlotte Rampling's character walking her dog across a rural landscape. The static establishing shots allow a brief pause between the heightened emotions of the intervening scenes. They help to build tension. They play on the knowledge that a dramatic climax is approaching.

FILMMAKER'S TIP:
Warning: it's very easy to use the establishing shot badly, to slip into the realms of the TV sitcom. For example, a static shot of the exterior of a house and then directly cutting to the interior.

INTIMATE MOMENTS
Films such as the Brit drama *45 Years* use scale to add emotion to tiny actions.

16. Masters

'If I can play a scene in a master shot, I always prefer it. And the actors always prefer it. It's fun to look at on the screen, the actors get a chance to sink their teeth into something substantial, and it's economically helpful.'
— **WOODY ALLEN**

It's often the case that the rhythm of a scene is determined by the way it's edited. The master shot can provide an elegant alternative. It can also lend your film a sense of gravitas, scale and artistry. A single fluid sequence that captures a lot of information is sometimes referred to as a 'long take'. The dynamics are determined through the movement of elements within the frame, or by the movement of the camera itself. These shots often require intricate planning – they are like a contraption with many moving parts.

Does there need to be movement?

No! The master shot can be used as the foundation of a scene. It's the basic framework into which other elements, such as close-ups or inserts, can be added later.

The centrepiece of the British director Steve McQueen's film *Hunger* (2008) is a 17-minute seated conversation between two actors, Michael Fassbender and Liam Cunningham, filmed in a single, static take. The rhythm and texture of the scene are created entirely through dialogue. In choosing not to use inserts or more conventional means of coverage, McQueen forces the viewer to pay closer attention to nuance and to appreciate the visual information that's being given.

Compare the simplicity of that sequence with the bravura complexity of one of Martin Scorsese's most famous shots, the club entrance in his film *Goodfellas* (1990). As Ray Liotta's character Henry Hill seduces Lorraine Bracco's Karen, so the single, sweeping shot seduces us.

IT'S SHOWTIME
The dazzling master shot in Martin Scorsese's *Goodfellas*.

17. Two-shot

The two-shot is the name given to a shot that places two actors within the same frame. A three-shot would contain three actors, and so on …

A conversation covered by a shot of one person talking, followed by a 'reverse-shot' of the person listening or responding, is a conventional approach of classical moviemaking. It is all too standard practice for a conversation on film to find its rhythm through cutting or movement – the ubiquitous walk-'n'-talk – rather than through the careful staging of elements within the frame.

There's an old-fashioned elegance to the two-shot that is often neglected. The necessity of having to fit two people into the frame means the two-shot tends to sit further away from the subjects than the 'head and shoulders' framing of the shot/reverse-shot alternative. It allows a greater freedom of movement for the actors. Body language becomes a more integral part of the dialogue. It leaves less room for manipulation, but gives more independence to the actors and the way in which they interact with one another.

Look at Richard Linklater's *Before Sunrise* (1995) and its sequels *Before Sunset* (2004) and *Before Midnight* (2013), which detail the decades-spanning love affair between romantic drifters Céline (Julie Delpy) and Jesse (Ethan Hawke). Given that these three films are almost entirely composed of a series of conversations, they're a great way of studying different means of approaching scenes that are driven by dialogue.

FILMMAKER'S TIP:

A strong two-shot can prevent the need to cut. The movement of the shot itself is determined by where the actors are and their subsequent actions. You can create an internal rhythm through staging (where elements are placed within the frame) and repositioning instead.

TWO'S COMPANY
Top: two figures in *The Grand Budapest Hotel*. Bottom: multiple figures in *Seven Samurai*.

18. Crossing the line

Whatever you do, just don't cross the line.

The basic rules of filmmaking are there to be broken. Yet there's one that remains essential if you want to maintain a sense of space and of where objects or actors sit in relation to one another. If you accidentally 'cross the line', a strange disruption of a scene's geography occurs. This is known as the 180-degree rule.

At its most basic, think of 'the line' as one drawn between the eyes of two actors in a given space. This may not remain constant, especially if they're moving around. In order to maintain coherence within a scene, the camera must stay on the same side of this invisible line.

Keep perspective

Imagine … you're sitting in a theatre watching a scene play out on stage. Your perspective remains constant because your position never suddenly switches to the other side of the stage. Were you to move, this sudden shift in perspective would result in the effect of crossing the line. It's a rule that plays an important part when it comes to editing footage together. Look out for continuity. If a subject walks off screen to the right, they'll need to enter from the left. Otherwise it looks as though they're walking backwards and forwards, unless the story has shifted to a different location and time has passed within the story.

There are plenty of examples of filmmakers intentionally breaking the 180-degree rule to create a sense of disorientation. There is a moment in Satoshi Kon's animated masterpiece *Paprika* (2006) in which a character explicitly explains the rule of the line before the film proceeds to smash it to bits.

LINE IN THE SAND
A vital rule in retaining
the relationship between
camera and subject.

19. Geography

'Tell the audience there's a bomb under that table and it will go off in five minutes ...' — **ALFRED HITCHCOCK**

Mainstream action cinema has a blatant disregard for geography. It bites a thumb when it comes to dealing with the space in which a scene occurs. It's as if the camera is a free pass to expand or contract dimensions at will.

A viewer can only know where Point A is in relation to Point B if you show them. No blitzkrieg of cutting can mask spatial incoherence. Make sure that it's clear where objects are in relation to one another and the space that they inhabit.

Some of cinema's most exciting set pieces draw their tension from a well-established sense of place. It's like setting up a long line of dominoes before having the satisfaction of seeing them tumble down.

Setting things up

Take the T. Rex attack from Steven Spielberg's *Jurassic Park*, for example. Notice the way that Spielberg takes his time setting up the scene. He familiarises the viewer with the position of all the actors and objects. There are no rapid cuts. It's classical in its presentation. Eye-lines determine movement, and the inclusion of another jeep in the background connects the two spaces. It ensures familiarity with its position relative to the first jeep, and the remainder of the set.

Spielberg does the same thing with a bomb sequence in *Munich* (2005). The device has been planted in an apartment. We're shown the position of the protagonists waiting outside, watching the upstairs window as they wait for a cue to set off the explosion. We know where everything is and how this should play out. Then Spielberg introduces a rogue element: the young daughter of the would-be victim. Now it's a race against the clock to stop the bomb. We know the distance the character has to cover in order to stop the explosion in time. Tension is generated by a pre-existing knowledge of the landscape.

DA BOMB
Spielberg's *Munich* offers a masterclass in space and geography.

20. Movement

Bring dynamism and energy to your film by moving the camera carefully. But even the smallest movement is loaded with meaning, so make it count.

Back in the early days of cinema, movie cameras were giant, immovable beasts. Now, given the size of today's digital cameras, mobility is no longer a problem. You can even strap a GoPro to a drone for the slickest aerial photography at negligible cost.

There's a brilliantly simple piece of 'objective' direction in Martin Scorsese's *Taxi Driver* (1976), that sees Robert De Niro's Travis Bickle talking on a payphone to his date. Travis has messed up with her and he's trying to make amends, but clearly not getting very far. Scorsese begins with his camera on Travis, a subjective shot that follows the attempt at conversation. Without warning, the camera slowly moves to the right, away from Travis, settling on an empty corridor that leads out to the street. It's a startlingly effective means of isolating the protagonist, of emphasising his loneliness. Even the camera isn't interested in him, it seems. Scorsese is explicitly commenting on his character with one simple move.

FILMMAKER'S TIP:

Be brutal with yourself when it comes to moving the camera. Remember that camera movement naturally implies subjectivity, for example, a character being following or watched. If the aim is for objectivity, look for ways to make a statement on the scene from the view of a detached outsider.

DRONING ON
Make sure every camera movement is fuelled by robust reasoning.

21. Zoom

The zoom was a staple of 1970s cinema. Today, it is largely used ironically or nostalgically.

A zoom is an artificial effect that can't be replicated by the human eye; not a camera move as such, merely an adjustment of the focal length of the lens. Objects can become enlarged, details can be clarified, and all with the flick of a thumb.

Get closer to the action

A zoom shot draws attention to the presence of the camera. It heightens the sense of realism, of the camera operator being physically present in the midst of the action. However, a word of caution: if you have only a smartphone at your disposal it's almost impossible to make a zoom action appear as an effortless glide. Zoom shots can look amazing, bringing a sense of cool voyeurism to a film. In his film *McCabe & Mrs. Miller* (1971), for instance, Robert Altman found many opportunities for an elegant zoom.

While zoom is a function available on all modern digital equipment, a simple dolly·or track can be laid to achieve a similar effect (see step 22) and may offer a less flamboyant visual solution.

The zoom can also be combined with the dolly shot to provide a heightened sense of anxiety or unease. By moving the camera away from the subject on dolly tracks while simultaneously zooming in, it's possible to achieve the unique visual effect made famous by Alfred Hitchcock in *Vertigo* (1958). The background of the shot appears to overwhelm the foreground, throwing the audience's sense of perspective off-balance. It's a neat visual shorthand for the James Stewart character's fear of heights.

FILMMAKER'S TIP:

Be aware that the zoom function on digital cameras will lead to a degradation in image quality, especially when used at night.

SNOW BUSINESS
The elegant zooms of Altman's *McCabe & Mrs. Miller.*

22. Dolly & truck

The decision to move a camera should not be taken lightly. But it will force you to think about how you can introduce exciting new elements into the frame.

Given their size, modern digital cameras are susceptible to the smallest vibrations. Our hands naturally tremble. The wind sways us from side to side. Achieving a perfectly still shot is a surprisingly difficult task (hint: use a tripod), but being aware of this fact will give your film an added air of professionalism. To move the camera smoothly, it's worthwhile investing in some basic tracks, which are readily and cheaply available online. Otherwise, improvise: attaching the camera to anything on wheels – for example, a skateboard or a shopping trolley – can work as a makeshift dolly. When making his nouvelle vague classic *Breathless* (1960), Jean-Luc Godard sat his cameraman in a wheelchair and physically pushed him around the streets and boudoirs of Paris.

What's the big difference?

The difference between a dolly shot and a truck shot is simply the direction in which the camera is moving. Dollies go forwards and backwards; trucks go from side to side. Both, to all intents and purposes, fall under the title of tracking shot.

A dolly shot differs from a zoom in that the focal length of your lens doesn't change as the camera itself physically moves towards or away from the subject. A zoom, by contrast, zeroes in on a specific piece of information within the frame without moving the camera. →

KEEPING ON BRANDO
The Godfather introduces its title character with an unforgettable dolly shot.

Think about the many ways in which a dolly shot might be used. A slow push-in on a character can lend a shot emotional weight by building a sense of intimacy with a subject, while a faster one might create a feeling of wonder or surprise – suggesting, for instance, a thought that hits the subject. And then, how does pulling away from a character change the shot's meaning?

Keep it smooth

A truck shot most commonly offers a means of following the subject. It's a way of moving the camera through a space in a smoother manner than if the shot were handheld.

A sequence in Park Chan-wook's film *Oldboy* (2003) sees its main character defending himself with a hammer from a horde of goons as the camera glides lengthways down the small corridor. It's a model of simplicity and elegance in the way it uses a truck shot to cover the unfolding action within a confined space.

The opening shot of Francis Ford Coppola's film *The Godfather* (1972) offers a stunning example of how to impart information gradually through a dolly shot. What begins as a close-up of an undertaker's monologue slowly pulls back to reveal the space he's sitting in: the Godfather's office. Our focus on the character speaking shifts to questions about the man listening as the dolly brings him into the side of the frame from behind. The close-up becomes a two-shot. The listener is the frame's dominant figure and the status of the two characters made clear. The speaker walks around the table to create a second two-shot before a cut introduces Marlon Brando's protagonist properly. With one simple dolly, Coppola introduces three separate compositional elements: a close-up followed by a pair of two-shots, each communicating more information about the relationship between the two characters.

Watchlist #5

Observe some of cinema's most impressive long takes.

1. Touch of Evil
ORSON WELLES, 1958

A grim Mexican border war is brought to life with customary brio by Orson Welles, who kicks off proceedings with a terrifying tracking shot that is synched up with a bomb that's been planted in the boot of a car.

2. Gravity
ALFONSO CUARÓN, 2013

Tracking shots are used to emulate real time, though they don't necessarily need to be created in a single take. The opening of Alfonso Cuarón's space opus is an intricate patchwork of snippets that have been made to look like one 17-minute marvel.

3. Boogie Nights
PAUL THOMAS ANDERSON, 1997

Anderson employs a sinuous tracking shot as the opening gambit of his porn-industry extravaganza. It stands as the perfect example of introducing your entire ensemble of characters in a single, minutely choreographed swoop.

4. Weekend
JEAN-LUC GODARD, 1967

One of cinema's most famous tracking shots appears in Jean Luc-Godard's coruscating and surreal satire of societal downfall, in which a camera slowly pans alongside a violent traffic jam that snakes through the countryside.

5. I Am Cuba
MIKHAIL KALATOZOV, 1964

The awe-inspiring tracking shots in this melancholic elegy to pre-revolutionary Cuba are used to offer a sense of grand scale, as at one point a camera pulls back from a funeral procession, revealing thousands of mourners filling the streets.

23. Handheld

Just because there are some basic rules regarding composition and camera movement, it doesn't mean they can't be thrown out of the window.

Shooting handheld can lend a scene or an entire film a looseness and a sense of dramatic immediacy that are more associated with documentary filmmaking. Look at Paul Greengrass's *Bourne* films and you can see how a handheld camera generates close-quarters dynamism in an action sequence. The knife vs. rolled-up magazine fight between Matt Damon and the goon in *The Bourne Supremacy* (2004) keeps editing to a minimum. The energy derives from the handheld camera's presence right in the midst of the action. It feels as though it's unfolding live, in real time.

Shooting handheld for extended periods of time isn't without its practical complications. The image still needs a certain level of stability to prevent viewers from feeling seasick – which is exactly what happened to audiences sitting down to watch the innovative handheld horror *The Blair Witch Project* in 1999. If the scene takes place in a confined space, provide something on which the camera operator can rest their elbows. If this isn't possible, an extended camera strap placed around the neck, holding the device with arms fully extended, can aid stability.

Many digital cameras and lenses come equipped with image stabilisation settings, which can be more effective than attempting to fix problems in post-production. Don't use a zoom lens: the wider the angle, the less shake you'll get on your image.

FILMMAKER'S TIP:
Watch out for horizontal lines in the image. Keeping the floor or the horizon level within the shot will ensure a balanced composition, even as you're moving.

BOURNE FREE
Up close and personal with the stars of *The Bourne Supremacy*.

24. Inside

Choosing to shoot your film indoors is a way to retain total control of what makes it into each frame. It also allows you to break out the lighting rig ...

Filming inside allows greater control of the shooting environment than filming outside. That's why most classic-era movies (and a fair few modern ones, too) are made on sound stages instead of on location. One of the key elements you can control is lighting. Electric lighting has a different colour temperature depending on the way you capture it. What appears as a neutral, white light to the naked eye can take on an undesirable yellow hue when filtered through a lens. Different bulbs provide different temperatures, so experiment before you shoot. As a general rule, fluorescent bulbs will be softer than LEDs, which are softer than regular household incandescent bulbs. It can be difficult to distinguish between the different bulbs at a glance, so check the labelling on the bulb itself.

If a subject is standing in front of a window, chances are high that the background will be over-exposed or the subject under-exposed, which means you'll lose detail on the subject's features. Keep the light source behind the camera, illuminating the object or person being filmed. Reflectors can bounce the light to the desired location if space is at a premium. You don't necessarily need a big fold-out reflector to get the job done. Even professionals use a sheet of polystyrene or a piece of cardboard covered in silver foil as a simple alternative.

Quickfire lighting rules: interiors

- Don't use overhead lighting.
- Don't light the subject from below
  (unless you're attempting a specific effect).
- Avoid shadows on faces.
- The larger the light source, the softer the light will be.
- Turn off your camera's automatic white-balance setting –
  it takes away your control over the colour temperature
  of the space you're shooting.

LET THERE BE LIGHT
Enhance mood and
detail with careful
placement of lights.

25. Outside

There's no getting away from the fact that shooting outside leaves you at the mercy of the elements.

If you are filming during the day, the principal light source will be that big bulb in the sky. There are countless factors that will affect the quality of light, from the time of day to the sudden arrival of nuisance clouds. Check the weather forecast before kicking off a shoot. If possible, bend nature to your needs (and vice versa).

See the light

Consider the position of the sun lighting the scene if you want to capture two characters conversing across the table. An overcast day makes the scene much more straightforward to shoot, but if the sun is behind one of the characters, they'll be lit unevenly. The simplest solution would be to rotate the table 90 degrees, so that the sun is lighting both characters evenly. Otherwise you'll need to use reflectors to bounce the sunlight on to the unlit subject.

Control the environment

Watch out for background action. If the shot is wide and taking place in a public place, there must be consistency behind the subjects. Figures or objects appearing and disappearing between cuts will look very strange. Keep the shots reasonably tight. If the background is especially busy, consider a shallow-focus effect that keeps your subject in focus while reducing background information to a light blur. This technique is often used as a cheat when a film is set in the past.

The art of noise

Use a directional microphone to ensure that the only audio being picked up is the dialogue. If there are loud noises intermittently interrupting the scene, such as a passing car, wait for the sound to clear before continuing. A clean soundtrack is essential, and almost impossible to fix later.

OPEN SEASON
Film outside and choose
to take on the elements
with your camera.

26. Magic hour

Magic hour (or golden hour) refers to that short filming opportunity after sunrise or before sunset, when the sun is low in the sky.

It's when natural light is at its warmest and kindest, imbuing images with a golden glow and enveloping softness that's, well, kinda magical.

It's impossible to talk about magic hour without reference to one of American cinema's foremost reclusive auteurs, Terrence Malick. If you want to see the extraordinary lighting effects afforded by shooting only at certain times of day, his film *Days of Heaven* (1978) is essential. Notice the warm halo that seems to surround the characters as they move through the cornfields.

Fire in the sky

If a film is made up mostly of exteriors and you're after a certain temperature to your images, along with soft textures and elongated shadows, you'll only find it away from the harsh light of day. It goes without saying that magic-hour photography will add extraordinary time constraints to a shooting schedule. Don't think it's possible to hate something as seemingly innocuous as a cloud? You will.

If you find yourself running out of time, or need to add additional shots at a later date, there are ways to re-create the magic-hour effect. A number of digital filters are available online, simple apps that can add that sun-kissed glow to an image.

FILMMAKER'S TIP

Find out your shooting window in advance – it's simple enough to find out online what time the sun sets. Prepare for constantly shifting levels of light that can prove a continuity nightmare. Allow more shooting days than you might think you need, reviewing each day's footage as you go.

FIELD OF DREAMS
Terrence Malick's *Days of Heaven* is the ultimate magic-hour movie.

27. Night

One of the great advantages of using a digital camera is its ability to capture detail in low-light settings.

A manual digital camera – with its ability to change lenses and ISO levels – will provide more reliable results than a smartphone, especially in low light. ISO is the setting that handles a camera's sensitivity to light. The lower the ISO number, the more light required to shoot.

With a DSLR, play around with the ISO settings, bearing in mind that the higher the ISO, the more pixelated the image will become. Even the most inexpensive cameras can handle up to ISO 1600 – or even 3200 – without too much degradation of the image. Using a lens with a shallow depth of field will make life a lot easier. Don't worry if you don't have access to a DSLR; shooting on a phone doesn't prevent you from filming at night, but the shooting environment may have to be managed more carefully.

Control the exposure

Most phones have a tendency to automate settings such as focus and exposure, which becomes especially problematic when moving the camera in low-light conditions. There are, however, budget-priced apps that allow greater control of certain elements, not least exposure, shutter speed and ISO settings.

FILMMAKER'S TIP:

When choosing the location for a night-time scene, find somewhere that has light sources already in place. Using a battery-powered LED attached to your camera can create an artificial effect and draw attention to the presence of the camera itself.

WITCHING HOUR
The Blair Witch Project
is a masterclass in the
lo-fi night shoot.

28. Driving

Address questions of safety before even beginning to think about the different ways of shooting a scene in a moving vehicle.

If, even for a second, you feel that safety might be compromised, forget it. Ditch the shot. Rework it. Set it on a bus.

Ask these questions: does the scene contain dialogue? Does the camera even need to be in the vehicle? Can the car be shot from a vehicle that's tailing? If a driver and a passenger are engaged in conversation, the only option without an expensive rig is to shoot from the back seat. Safety concerns will arise if you're wielding a camera in the driver's face, so think about interesting ways of using the car mirrors to capture faces through inserts or cutaways.

While your camera may be small enough to mount on the car dashboard, the fixed perspective offers few possibilities for variation. Driving scenes shot by day can prove a nightmare for continuity, given the ever-changing background information. Shooting in a car by night also brings up a plethora of lighting concerns. Keeping your camera close to your subjects and using a shallow depth of field can reduce background interference.

The illusion of speed

The introduction of the protagonists in the Coen brothers' debut feature *Blood Simple* (1984) offers a straightforward example of how to keep things, well, simple. It's a dialogue scene shot from the back seat of a seemingly moving car, but the vehicle is in fact stationary. The combination of rain on the windscreen and moving lights obscures any giveaway details and gives the impression of a vehicle in motion.

The great Iranian filmmaker, Abbas Kiarostami made an entire film out of driving scenes. *Ten* (2002) was shot using a camera fixed to a dashboard as a woman picks up various passengers around Tehran. The elegant simplicity of its design was made possible only through the size of modern digital cameras, and the possibilities they allow for improvisation.

KINGS OF THE ROAD
Driving shots can be a tough prospect for the micro-budget filmmaker.

29. On the lam

If there's a shot you absolutely, positively have to get but you don't have the financial resources for it, throw caution to the wind and go guerilla.

Shooting a film in a public space requires the permission of the council or local authority. Filming permits can vary in cost, depending on the space required for the shoot. Check to see if it's possible to negotiate a deal, as there are sometimes contingencies for low-budget projects.

Even when filming on a residential street, it's important to inform those who live there of your plans. Besides being a courtesy, it offers you a better shot at controlling the shooting environment.

Densely populated areas can be a nightmare to shoot while maintaining control of background action. Faces peering down the lens of the camera can make a shot unusable. Think about how necessary it is for a scene to take place in a specific location. Watch out for unwanted product placement, too: you don't want to find yourself liable for payment if you accidentally include a brand logo prominently in your shot.

On the run

In *Band of Outsiders* (1964), Jean-Luc Godard filmed a scene in which his characters dash through the Louvre in Paris by simply sneaking his camera in and getting his actors to make a run for it. The security guards chasing the cast in the scene are those who were on duty that day. This is a guerilla tactic that does not bear repeating.

It's a time-consuming necessity to ensure that the relevant permissions are in place for filming in a public space. Consider whether it's worth rewriting scenes to limit locations to private properties that won't create any logistical or legal problems.

DASH CAM
Top: Godard's *Band of Outsiders*. Bottom: the cold reality of their antics.

30. Continuity

The smallest continuity error can drag an audience straight out of a scene and undermine credibility.

It can be traumatic to design and shoot the most beautifully constructed sequence, a series of shots that form the emotional climax of the film, only to arrive in the edit and discover a glaring error. The actor is wearing a tie in one shot but not the next. His performance may be terrific, but the only thing noticeable is the disappearing act performed by the offending garment.

While a filmed sequence creates the illusion of taking place in real time, each shot is created individually, perhaps not even on the same day. As actions are repeated – either by the actor or by the camera – there must be consistency for the shots to cut together seamlessly when it comes to editing the film.

Keep it all together

Everything needs to be considered, and a record must be kept. This is where the script supervisor comes in. They will maintain a log of all the important information taking place within a scene. If actions are being performed, they'll be described in detail. Likewise the use of props. Did the actor pick up the phone with the left or right hand?

Without a script supervisor on hand, it's just one more thing that needs attention. Use a phone to take photographs of the cast wardrobe at the beginning and end of a scene. Likewise the dressing of the set. If a sequence isn't completed in a single day, it's worth reviewing the footage with the cast before the rest is shot or re-shot, to ensure that they remember the specifics of their actions and movements.

FILMMAKER'S TIP:

The more detailed the continuity report, the more accurately everything can be replicated across multiple shots, reducing the risk of discovering jarring errors when it's too late to fix them.

SPOT THE DIFFERENCE
Chaplin's iconic Little Tramp is trapped in a continuity nightmare.

31. Cutaways

Give your action poetic context by looking to the bounty of the wider world. Consider cutaways as punctuation, or a moment to catch a breath.

Even if a scene is planned out, there is always room to improvise on the day by adding a little texture when it comes to the edit.

A few takes can capture all manner of details. Small gestures can be integrated into a sequence later on. This is often referred to as 'B-roll'. These shots can last for one or many seconds and don't necessarily need to provide narrative information, either.

A famous example of a type of shot that can bring weight to a scene without altering its narrative content is the Pillow Shot, which gets its name from a type of shot made by the great Japanese filmmaker Yasujiro Ozu. They were often quite literally shots of pillows or other inanimate objects lasting several seconds, used as a kind of cinematic punctuation, a cushioning of the surrounding drama.

Ozu didn't just randomly insert literal shots of pillows into his films, however. The definition extends to cutaways of landscapes or vacant spaces that have a similar function to the establishing shot, a visual non sequitur that allows a contemplative rhythm to be established. Spare some time in the shooting schedule to capture seemingly extraneous details since they can benefit the construction of a sequence later.

Such shots can emphasise the meaning of a scene, but they can also undermine it. Don't kill the impact of a dramatically important scene with a cutaway to a nonplussed cat.

FILMMAKER'S TIP:

Once a scene's dramatic information has been captured, run another take that focuses on smaller elements, such as gesture. Perhaps the way a character holds their hands, or the rain falling against a window.

TALKING JAPANESE
Yasujiro Ozu is famous for atmospheric 'pillow' shots between scenes.

32. Recording dialogue

It's easy to visualise the images of a prospective movie in our head, but imagining how it might sound is a far tougher prospect.

Sound is important. Don't underestimate how important. It's easy to get away with a lot when it comes to the quality of the image, but sound is far less forgiving. While a modern smartphone has the capability of capturing great images, it's unlikely that its built-in microphone will get the job done, especially when shooting outside. An ultra-directional microphone becomes an essential piece of kit, one that can focus on a much narrower range.

    The more confined the shooting environment, the easier the sound will be to control. Background noise is to be avoided at all costs. It'll constantly change from take to take, and it'll be impossible to cut the final footage together without jarring shifts. It's much better to add a separately recorded background track in post-production that flows across the edits. →

FILMMAKER'S TIP:
Study every location for light requirements in advance, but also study every location for sound requirements. Every space will react differently when dialogue is recorded, so it's important to work out how best to achieve a clean recording, free from reverb.

SOUND ADVICE
Francis Ford Coppola's *The Conversation* is about capturing and manipulating sound.

Music within a scene

Capturing music at the same time as your dialogue causes problems when there's a cut. Remember, these elements can always be added during the edit, but can't be taken away if they're on the recording.

Professional productions use clapperboards as simultaneous visual and audio cues from which to synch the sound. You don't need an actual clapperboard, though – just get someone to stand in front of the camera at the start of the shot and demonstrably clap their hands together.

If you are capturing dialogue during a scene that involves lots of movement, rehearsal becomes a necessity. Whoever is holding the boom (a microphone on the end of a pole) must be aware of the position of the top of frame to avoid appearing in shot.

FILMMAKER'S TIP:

If a dedicated sound recordist is an expense too far, it's important to check the sound on the day. Don't listen to the dialogue being spoken live, wear headphones connected to the sound equipment to give you an accurate indication of what's being recorded.

Watchlist #6

A shortlist of cinema's great audio innovators.

1. The Exorcist
WILLIAM FRIEDKIN, 1973

This punishing tale of a woman attempting to save her daughter from demonic possession creates chills from simple off-camera sounds, such as the constant scuttle of 'rats' in the attic.

2. A Man Escaped
ROBERT BRESSON, 1956

A French resistance fighter attempts to break out of prison in Robert Bresson's existential masterpiece. The subject's desire for freedom is enhanced by the cacophony of sounds that emanate from outside his small cell.

3. Berberian Sound Studio
PETER STRICKLAND, 2012

Although this superb British oddity boasts impeccable sound design in its own right, it also tells the story of a misbegotten foley artist and his descent into the audio nightmare of 1970s Italian gore flicks.

4. M
FRITZ LANG, 1931

One of the first and still one of the best ever serial-killer movies, Fritz Lang's M links the identity of a child-murderer to a short whistled refrain that pops up amid the silences on the film's exemplary soundtrack.

5. Trainspotting
DANNY BOYLE, 1996

Sometimes a good pop track and some canny beat-matched editing is all it takes to create an evocative cinematic experience, and this is exemplified in Danny Boyle's pounding, Britpop-era drug addiction comedy.

33. Ambient sound

A film can live or die by the quality of its audio. Take measures to get the small things right and allow room to stack up levels of atmospheric, ambient sound.

While we've already seen the need for clean dialogue recording, there are other sound elements that deserve attention. A dedicated sound person would use a field mixer as a means of capturing the film's audio backdrop – all sound that isn't dialogue. This piece of kit allows the sound levels to be adjusted carefully during recording. Otherwise, the microphone is likely to be jacked directly into the camera itself.

Bear in mind, however, that capturing your audio separately from the video with a simple sound recorder allows greater control over audio levels. Run some volume tests prior to the first take to check that the sound levels aren't peaking, because any distortion will render the recordings useless.

For interior scenes, capture what's known as a room tone. Make a recording of the space in which the scene is taking place, with nobody talking. Let the audio run for a few minutes. Adding this room tone track underneath the scene at a low volume during the sound mix will mask any minor sound fluctuations that appear in the edit.

The same applies to exterior scenes. When filming dialogue outside, use a directional mic that cuts out any background noise. The idea is to capture the dialogue as cleanly as possible. A separately recorded ambient or 'wild' track can be laid under the scene during the mix for a seamless transition between edits.

FILMMAKER'S TIP:

A directional (or shotgun) microphone is an essential tool for recording dialogue, as is a stereo microphone for ambient or background effects.

ROCK THE MIC
Shotgun, tie clip, radio ... Pick the right mic for your needs.

Post

34. Organising

With all your footage in the can, it's tempting to jump straight into the edit. But it really pays to spend some time organising the material first.

First things first: save and back up everything. Then check that everything's properly saved and backed up. Now it's time to turn those hundreds of shots and takes into an actual movie.

Before importing the hours of video into the editing software you plan to use, create a series of folders to label and categorise your footage. Knowing the location of every single shot and insert will ensure the edit runs smoothly. Return to the shooting script and create a folder for each scene. Into each folder, place the relevant video and audio clips, labelling them with the type of shot and the take number (e.g. Master 01).

If the sound has been recorded separately from the video, it must be paired up with the relevant images. This will take a long time, but will make the process of cutting everything together much less painstaking once it's done. It will also enable the best selection of footage; there's nothing worse than finding a great shot only to discover that the soundtrack makes it worthless. It can be a tedious process, but proper footage management will save a lot of headaches in the long run. Also, keeping everything in a single place allows ease of access and spontaneity in the editing room.

FILMMAKER'S TIP:

Don't get rid of anything. You never know what you might want to source from a single take, even if there are obvious mistakes. Just because an actor bumps into a table doesn't mean there isn't a usable moment that's unique to that one take.

YOU GOTTA HAVE A SYSTEM
John Cusack in *High Fidelity*, cataloguing his vast vinyl collection.

35. Selecting material

Be brutal. Try to think of your film project as a living, breathing being that requires perfect equilibrium to thrive. Make sure all footage serves a wider purpose.

Working through every single shot of a scene, make notes on the various elements worth including. What are the pros and cons of each take? Which contains the best performance?

Don't feel that a take must be used in its entirety. The great thing about the magic of the editing process is the ability to pull the best elements from different sources and stitch them together to create something new and special.

Mix and match

If the sound recording is strong on one particular take, but the visuals aren't up to scratch, think of ways you can use that soundtrack with visual elements from different takes. By cutting to reaction shots, for example, you can keep the sound of the person talking while using images from elsewhere. It may be the case that entire sequences are completely unusable, for either technical or narrative reasons.

Peter Jackson famously released extended editions of each film in his *Lord of the Rings* trilogy a year after their initial release. There was nothing wrong with the scenes that were excluded from the theatrical cuts on a technical level, they simply slowed down the momentum of the film. →

MY PRECIOUS
Peter Jackson, making
his streamlined versions
of *The Lord of the Rings*.

Making the cut

A huge argument during the editing process of William Friedkin's *The Exorcist* (1973) meant that the director and the writer, William Peter Blatty, didn't speak for years. The scene in question centred on a discussion between the two priests that set out the film's key themes. While Blatty wanted these themes to be stated explicitly, Friedkin argued for ambiguity by omitting the scene. Only in 2000 was the scene reinstated by Friedkin as a favour to the writer.

It can be hard to maintain an objective eye on the material when you've been staring at the same footage for days on end. If in doubt, get a second opinion. Show collaborators or friends different versions of a sequence to get their honest opinion on what should stay and what should go. A small, trusted audience can be valuable even at this stage of proceedings.

FILMMAKER'S TIP:

The effort to capture a certain shot on the day means nothing now. All that matters is whether that shot serves the scene or not. If it doesn't, bin it. Be ruthless. Kill your darlings.

Watchlist #7

Or, recut your movie until it works for you.

1. Apocalypse Now Redux
FRANCIS FORD COPPOLA, 2001

An unfinished cut of this Vietnam war epic managed to win the Palme d'Or at the 1979 Cannes Film Festival, but Coppola and sound editor Walter Murch assembled an extended, re-edited cut of the ultimate bad-trip movie in 2001.

2. Brazil
TERRY GILLIAM, 1985

Owing to disagreements between its director and the US distributors of the film, this dark, dystopian satire was set to feature a specially filmed happy ending as a way to connect to American audiences. Terry Gilliam fought for (and eventually won) the right to release his preferred cut of the film.

3. Blade Runner: The Final Cut
RIDLEY SCOTT, 2007

Ridley Scott's grandiose neo noir, adapted from a Philip K. Dick novel, is an example of a film that has been constantly tinkered with and 'improved' since its original release in 1982. This is one of seven versions of the film ...

4. Miami Vice
MICHAEL MANN, 2006

Sometimes, a home-entertainment release can be used as a way for a director to make a minor but important personal tweak to a movie. Michael Mann's DVD cut of Miami Vice adds an extra song to the soundtrack, linking the film back to the original TV property.

5. Donnie Darko: The Director's Cut
RICHARD KELLY, 2004

An example of how less can sometimes be more. Richard Kelly's extended cut of this cult sci-fi hit features reams of unnecessary information and poor-quality effects work – material that should've hit the edit room floor.

36. Rhythm

*'A film is – or should be – more like music than fiction.
It should be a progression of moods and feelings.
The theme, ... the meaning, all that comes later.'*
— **STANLEY KUBRICK**

As a rule of thumb, the editing of a film isn't something to draw attention to. It can be used to create pace and drama, but it must also remain invisible so as not to draw the viewer out of the scene.

Always consider the length of each shot and its sequencing in relation to another. Moving from one shot to another must make sense, both narratively and spatially. There are different ways you can craft a transition between scenes.

The jump cut

This is a harsh, jarring effect that takes the viewer somewhere unexpected. In *Lawrence of Arabia* (1962), David Lean shows Peter O'Toole in his superior's office, having just received his orders. He holds a lit match between his fingers. The split-second he blows out the match, Lean jump-cuts to the desert horizon. It is a simple, magnificent transition to the other side of the world.

The wipe

An old-fashioned effect that sees one image scroll across the screen over another, effectively wiping it out and taking its place. George Lucas uses such a device throughout his *Star Wars* series, replicating the wipes from the early 1930s serials, such as *Flash Gordon* and *Buck Rogers*, which he so admired. →

MATCH CUTTING
Lawrence of Arabia,
with perhaps the
greatest single cut
in all cinema.

The fade to black

Fading into a black screen then out of it into the next scene can be an effective means of demonstrating the passing of time, but it will slow your transitions down, affecting the overall pacing of the film.

Rules can't be broken until the basics are mastered

For the first pass at a cut of the film, keep things simple. Start off with a basic assembly. Don't worry about the length of each shot for now, just make sure the scenes make visual and narrative sense. If two people are talking while the film cuts between them, is one of them suddenly standing in a different part of the room when we next see them? There must be a means of showing how they got there.

This part of the edit is intuitive. A mistake or disruption in continuity stands out like a sore thumb. Once the basic assembly of a sequence is in place, start fine-tuning each shot individually. Play around with the lengths of different shots. If they're all the same length, the lack of rhythm in the scene will be immediately apparent. Experiment with how cutting on movement affects a scene's fluidity.

Again, there are no hard-and-fast rules. Many decisions will be instinctive. Once each individual scene has been tackled, step back and see how it works within the context of the film as a whole. Some sequences may stop the film dead in its tracks. Get rid of them. Some may offer the opportunity to slow things down for a few minutes.

Don't just think about the rhythm of each individual scene. Think about how the rhythm of each scene affects the entire film.

Watchlist #8

How to build a movie, one tiny brick at a time.

1. Psycho
ALFRED HITCHCOCK, 1960

*Not only is this Hitchcock classic oddly structured with its two-tier story,
it also boasts an editing masterclass in the classic shower scene, which
contains 78 different camera set-ups and took seven days to film.*

2. Battleship Potemkin
SERGEI EISENSTEIN, 1925

*Along with his collaborator Grigori Aleksandrov, director Sergei Eisenstein
is considered responsible for coining all manner of editing techniques in this
barnstorming silent re-creation of a naval uprising in the port of Odessa.*

3. Uncle Boonmee Who Can Recall His Past Lives
APICHATPONG WEERASETHAKUL, 2010

*This lyrical Thai prizewinner about ghosts, doubles, political unrest and a
catfish princess achieves greatness via the simple process of offering a visual
and sonic surprise with every cut.*

4. Breathless
JEAN-LUC GODARD, 1960

*Testament to the fact that the rule book is there to be torn up, Breathless
saw Jean-Luc Godard redefining film rhythm by employing the jump cut to
give a snappy, carefree rhythm to his story of a romantic
rogue on the run in Paris.*

5. High Noon
FRED ZINNEMANN, 1952

*This seminal paranoia Western, in which a soon-to-retire marshal played by
Gary Cooper awaits his destiny as the clock ticks in the background, uses
editing as a kind of metronome to signify the inexorable passing of time.*

37. Music

Underscore the emotion of a scene with music, or use it as a counterpoint, a means of commenting on the action without stating it through dialogue or image.

Avoid being too literal. There's nothing more toe-curling than the lyrics of a song explicitly stating the point of a scene. Or worse, stating it nonsensically. LL Cool J's odd references to the Titanic and shark-based headwear ('Uh, my hat is like a shark's fin/Deepest, bluest, my hat is like a shark's fin') bear little resemblance to anything seen on screen in *Deep Blue Sea* (1999).

A recurrent emotional touchstone can be created with a returning musical motif. Look at the way directors use the James Bond theme throughout the series. Familiarity with the music creates a sense of excitement, an amplification of an action sequence. When the theme kicks in, we know Bond means business.

Keep it legal

It's important to be aware of the legal issues surrounding the use of other people's music in a film. Obtaining clearance rights for a well-known song can prove prohibitively expensive.

You don't need to be or know a composer to score a film. There's plenty of music that's either in the public domain or available to license. Don't rule out the possibility of contacting musicians directly to work out an agreement for the use of their music; it's a shared opportunity for exposure that works both ways. Above all, be aware that music can be an extremely powerful tool. Used precisely and sparingly, it can elevate a scene beyond the sum of its parts. Used bluntly or as a shortcut to emotion, it can ruin what's readily apparent without it.

FILMMAKER'S TIP:

Music enhances what's already there. If the actors and filmmaking have done the heavy lifting, there's no need to force a point.

JUMPING THE SHARK
Or when music selections go bad in the film *Deep Blue Sea*.

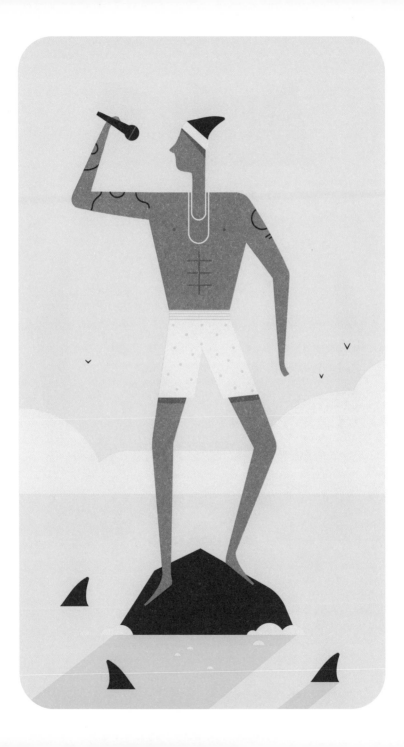

38. Finishing touches

Once the editing process is complete, it's time to make a finished copy of the film.

Titles at the start of the film and a complete list of credits at the end are easily added. Make sure every single member of the production is given their due, no matter how small their role. If they're not being paid for their time and work, a credit can make a huge difference. If money for the film has been raised through crowdsourcing, consider adding the names of the contributors.

There's no need to fret about complex file formats or issues of compatibility, since most editing software now comes with handy single-click solutions. Once the picture has been locked, it's simply a case of scrolling down a tab and selecting the ideal screening platform for you – this could range from burning a film directly on to a Blu-ray, transferring it to a USB drive or posting directly to an online viewing platform. The software will also automatically make sure that your film is optimised with regard to potentially fiddly variables such as resolution and aspect ratio.

Platforms such as YouTube or Vimeo allow you to upload the project and protect it with a password, making it easy to share with friends and colleagues without the hassle and expense of sending out physical media. This is also great for applying to film festivals.

FILMMAKER'S TIP:
It's useful to have different means of playing the completed film, depending on where and how you plan to screen it. For amateur filmmakers, it's vital to make a copy to be viewed online – the primary mode of delivery for this type of work.

SCREENING CONDITIONS
It's time to get your movie project out into the big wide world.

39. Finding an audience

Finishing the movie is just the start of the journey.
The work of connecting the film to an audience is the
next exciting challenge.

So, you've made a film! All those weeks – months, even – of blood,
sweat and tears. Now's the opportunity to get the finished work in
front of an audience. Of course, you owe it to the cast and crew to
put on a screening of the finished film. If you've raised money for
the project through friends and family, make sure you give them an
opportunity to see their money up on the screen. If you're nervous
about how the film might be received, show it to some trusted friends
or collaborators first. It's never too late to make changes before you
show it to a bigger audience.

Screen the film

Find a local bar with a big screen. Tell them you'll be packing the
place out with a drink-buying rabble for the night and they'll probably
give you the space for free. Get on social media. Invite all and sundry
to come to see how hard you've been working all these months.
Provide popcorn.

You'll have made a number of great new contacts and creative
partnerships in the process of making your film. Now that you've got
your first movie under your belt, go out and make some more. This is
your calling card. Find a local networking event for amateur or semi-
professional filmmakers. There are more and more film festivals that
screen local work. Many offer free submissions, and an opportunity to
put your work in front of a wider audience.

- Get out there.
- Take your film with you.
- Show it to the world ... then get started on
  that difficult second album!

WORLD PREMIERE
Screen your film, and
then get thinking about
what you'll do next.

Resources

BUDGETING

Title _____

Length _____

Producer _____

Director _____

Budget date _____

CAST

Actors _____ _____

Extras _____ _____

Cast Total _____ _____

CREW

Writer _____ _____

Director _____ _____

Producer _____ _____

Storyboard artist _____ _____

Production designer _____ _____

Set builders _____ _____

Costume designer _____ _____

Production manager _____ _____

Director of photography _____ _____

Camera operator _____ _____

Camera assistant _____ _____

Sound recordist _____ _____

Boom operator _____ _____

Gaffer _____ _____

Grips _____ _____

Hair/make-up artist _____ _____

Production assistant/driver _____ _____

Editor _____ _____

Sound designer _____ _____

Mixer _____ _____

Musicians _____ _____

Crew Total _____ _____

PRE-PRODUCTION

Transportation (scouting) _____ _____

Rehearsal space _____ _____

Casting _____ _____

Research _____ _____

Pre-production Total _____ _____

112

Number of weeks

Days per week

Pre-production starts/ends

Production starts/ends

Post-production starts/ends

PRODUCTION

Cameras, lenses

Grips

Lights

Sound

Supplies (gels, diffusion, gaffer tape, etc.)

Hard drives, memory cards, tapes

Studio/location rental

Set construction

Set dressing

Props

Costumes (including cleaning)

Hair styling and make-up

Special FX

Transportation (rental, fuel, parking)

Meals

Accommodation

Production stills

Insurance

Production Total

POST-PRODUCTION

Editing space

Computers, hard drives

Editing software

DVDs

Stock music

Mixing

Colour grading

Mastering

DVD copies

Packaging

Promotion and festival fees

Post-production Total

Contingency 10%

GRAND TOTAL

Title	
Length	
Producer	
Director	
Budget date	

CAST

Actors	
Extras	

Cast Total

CREW

Writer	
Director	
Producer	
Storyboard artist	
Production designer	
Set builders	
Costume designer	
Production manager	
Director of photography	
Camera operator	
Camera assistant	
Sound recordist	
Boom operator	
Gaffer	
Grips	
Hair/make-up artist	
Production assistant/driver	
Editor	
Sound designer	
Mixer	
Musicians	

Crew Total

PRE-PRODUCTION

Transportation (scouting)	
Rehearsal space	
Casting	
Research	

Pre-production Total

Number of weeks

Days per week

Pre-production starts/ends

Production starts/ends

Post-production starts/ends

PRODUCTION

Cameras, lenses

Grips

Lights

Sound

Supplies (gels, diffusion, gaffer tape, etc.)

Hard drives, memory cards, tapes

Studio/location rental

Set construction

Set dressing

Props

Costumes (including cleaning)

Hair styling and make-up

Special FX

Transportation (rental, fuel, parking)

Meals

Accommodation

Production stills

Insurance

Production Total

POST-PRODUCTION

Editing space

Computers, hard drives

Editing software

DVDs

Stock music

Mixing

Colour grading

Mastering

DVD copies

Packaging

Promotion and festival fees

Post-production Total

Contingency 10%

GRAND TOTAL

SHOOTING SCHEDULE

Production title		Breakfast time	
Shoot date		Lunch time	
Crew call		Weather	
Wrap time		Nearest hospital	

SCENE	INT/EXT	DAY/NIGHT	SET	LOCATION	CONTACT	PAGE COUNT

CAST	CHARACTER	MAKE-UP/HAIR	COSTUME	READY

DEPARTMENT	TITLE	NAME	PHONE	CALL TIME

SPECIAL REQUIREMENTS

KEY CONTACTS	NAME	PHONE	EMAIL
PRODUCER			
PRODUCTION MANAGER			
FIRST ASSISTANT DIRECTOR			

SHOOTING SCHEDULE

Production title		Breakfast time	
Shoot date		Lunch time	
Crew call		Weather	
Wrap time		Nearest hospital	

SCENE	INT/EXT	DAY/NIGHT	SET	LOCATION	CONTACT	PAGE COUNT

CAST		CHARACTER	MAKE-UP/HAIR	COSTUME	READY

DEPARTMENT	TITLE	NAME	PHONE	CALL TIME

SPECIAL REQUIREMENTS

KEY CONTACTS	NAME	PHONE	EMAIL
PRODUCER			
PRODUCTION MANAGER			
FIRST ASSISTANT DIRECTOR			

SHOOTING SCHEDULE

Production title		Breakfast time	
Shoot date		Lunch time	
Crew call		Weather	
Wrap time		Nearest hospital	

SCENE	INT/EXT	DAY/NIGHT	SET	LOCATION	CONTACT	PAGE COUNT

CAST	CHARACTER	MAKE-UP/HAIR	COSTUME	READY

DEPARTMENT	TITLE	NAME	PHONE	CALL TIME

SPECIAL REQUIREMENTS

KEY CONTACTS	NAME	PHONE	EMAIL
PRODUCER			
PRODUCTION MANAGER			
FIRST ASSISTANT DIRECTOR			

SHOOTING SCHEDULE

Production title _____   Breakfast time _____
Shoot date _____   Lunch time _____
Crew call _____   Weather _____
Wrap time _____   Nearest hospital _____

SCENE	INT/EXT	DAY/NIGHT	SET	LOCATION	CONTACT	PAGE COUNT

CAST	CHARACTER	MAKE-UP/HAIR	COSTUME	READY

DEPARTMENT	TITLE	NAME	PHONE	CALL TIME

SPECIAL REQUIREMENTS

_____
_____
_____

KEY CONTACTS	NAME	PHONE	EMAIL
PRODUCER			
PRODUCTION MANAGER			
FIRST ASSISTANT DIRECTOR			

EQUIPMENT CHECKLIST

Production title _____

Shoot date _____

VIDEO

- [ ] Camera
- [ ] _____ mm lens
- [ ] _____ mm lens
- [ ] _____ mm lens
- [ ] Camera batteries
- [ ] Camera battery charger
- [ ] Camera power adapter
- [ ] Video tapes/Cards/Hard drives
- [ ] Camera rods
- [ ] Matte box
- [ ] ND filter
- [ ] Vario ND filter
- [ ] _____ filter
- [ ] _____ filter
- [ ] Follow focus
- [ ] Video monitor
- [ ] Monitor batteries
- [ ] Monitor battery charger
- [ ] Slate
- [ ] Tripod
- [ ] Tripod plate
- [ ] Lens cleaning equipment
- [ ] Camera bag
- [ ] White card

AUDIO

- [ ] Shotgun microphone
- [ ] Shockmount
- [ ] Windjammer
- [ ] Boom
- [ ] Microphone stand
- [ ] Lavalier microphones
- [ ] Wireless transmitter
- [ ] Wireless receiver
- [ ] Headphones
- [ ] Field mixer
- [ ] Batteries

LIGHTING

- [ ] _____ light
- [ ] _____ light
- [ ] _____ light
- [ ] _____ stand
- [ ] _____ stand
- [ ] _____ stand
- [ ] _____ C-stand
- [ ] _____ C-stand
- [ ] _____ C-stand
- [ ] Spare bulbs
- [ ] Gels
- [ ] Diffusion
- [ ] Scrims
- [ ] Reflectors
- [ ] Gloves
- [ ] Clamps
- [ ] Misc grip equipment
- [ ] Sandbags

CABLES & ADAPTERS

- [ ] Camera charger cable
- [ ] Camera AC cable
- [ ] Monitor power cable
- [ ] XLR microphone cables
- [ ] Extension cords
- [ ] Adapters

MISC

- [ ] Gaffer tape
- [ ] Small toolkit, scissors
- [ ] Rope
- [ ] Make-up
- [ ] Still camera
- [ ] Small ladder
- [ ] Carrying cart
- [ ] Tape measure
- [ ] Batteries
- [ ] Paper
- [ ] Writing materials

EQUIPMENT CHECKLIST

Production title _____   Shoot date _____

VIDEO

- ☐ Camera
- ☐ _____ mm lens
- ☐ _____ mm lens
- ☐ _____ mm lens
- ☐ Camera batteries
- ☐ Camera battery charger
- ☐ Camera power adapter
- ☐ Video tapes/Cards/Hard drives
- ☐ Camera rods
- ☐ Matte box
- ☐ ND filter
- ☐ Vario ND filter
- ☐ _____ filter
- ☐ _____ filter
- ☐ Follow focus
- ☐ Video monitor
- ☐ Monitor batteries
- ☐ Monitor battery charger
- ☐ Slate
- ☐ Tripod
- ☐ Tripod plate
- ☐ Lens cleaning equipment
- ☐ Camera bag
- ☐ White card

AUDIO

- ☐ Shotgun microphone
- ☐ Shockmount
- ☐ Windjammer
- ☐ Boom
- ☐ Microphone stand
- ☐ Lavalier microphones
- ☐ Wireless transmitter
- ☐ Wireless receiver
- ☐ Headphones
- ☐ Field mixer
- ☐ Batteries

LIGHTING

- ☐ _____ light
- ☐ _____ light
- ☐ _____ light
- ☐ _____ stand
- ☐ _____ stand
- ☐ _____ stand
- ☐ _____ C-stand
- ☐ _____ C-stand
- ☐ _____ C-stand
- ☐ Spare bulbs
- ☐ Gels
- ☐ Diffusion
- ☐ Scrims
- ☐ Reflectors
- ☐ Gloves
- ☐ Clamps
- ☐ Misc grip equipment
- ☐ Sandbags

CABLES & ADAPTERS

- ☐ Camera charger cable
- ☐ Camera AC cable
- ☐ Monitor power cable
- ☐ XLR microphone cables
- ☐ Extension cords
- ☐ Adapters

MISC

- ☐ Gaffer tape
- ☐ Small toolkit, scissors
- ☐ Rope
- ☐ Make-up
- ☐ Still camera
- ☐ Small ladder
- ☐ Carrying cart
- ☐ Tape measure
- ☐ Batteries
- ☐ Paper
- ☐ Writing materials

Shot size is defined by the size of the human figure in the frame.

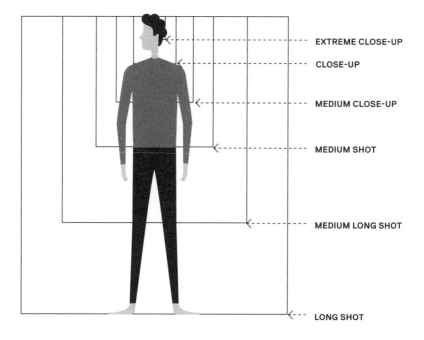

EXTREME CLOSE-UP

CLOSE-UP

MEDIUM CLOSE-UP

MEDIUM SHOT

MEDIUM LONG SHOT

LONG SHOT

TYPE	ABBREVIATION	DESCRIPTION
EXTREME CLOSE-UP	(ECU)	A shot that isolates a small detail, typically the eyes of a character.
CLOSE-UP	(CU)	A shot that emphasises a character's face or another body part. It can also be used to show an object isolated from its background.
MEDIUM CLOSE-UP	(MCU)	From head to chest.
MEDIUM SHOT	(MS)	From head to waist.
MEDIUM LONG SHOT	(MLS)	From head to just above the knees. (Avoid framing below the knees.)
LONG SHOT	(LS)	A shot that shows the whole human figure, from head to toe. May include a fair amount of background. Sometimes called a full shot.
EXTREME LONG SHOT	(ELS)	A very wide shot that shows where the scene takes place. Sometimes called an establishing shot. The focus is on the surroundings, not on the people who may appear in the shot.
MASTER SHOT	-	A shot that shows the entire scene, from beginning to end. (Usually a long shot.) The master shot is frequently used as a kind of safety shot that a director can go back to if something goes wrong. Some directors always do a master shot; others despise them.
TWO-SHOT, THREE-SHOT, GROUP SHOT	-	A shot that includes two, three or more characters.
OVER-THE-SHOULDER SHOT	(OS)	A shot that shows someone talking, with the person they are talking to visible at the edge of the frame.

Shooting script

The shooting script is an annotated script with lines running down the text to indicate shot size and what part of the scene is covered by each shot. Number the scenes and the shots.

```
17 -   EXT. DAY - LAKESIDE
                1 ⊤ LS
        It's a nice summer day. JOHN is walking alone by the
        lakeside. On a bench, a girl, ANN, is reading a book. He
        greets her from a distance.
                           2 ⊤ MS
                          JOHN
                Hi Ann. What are you reading?
                                        3 ⊤ MCU
                          ANN
                       (turning to him)
                Oh, hi John, I didn't see you
                coming. I'm reading a book about
                spiritual development.
                   4 ⊤ MCU
                        JOHN
                Sounds fascinating.
```

Shot list

Once you have finished the visual planning, make a list of all your shots. Use it during the shoot to ensure that you have all the shots you need to tell your story.

SCENE NO.	SHOT NO.	SHOT SIZE	LOCATION	DESCRIPTION
17	1	LS	Lakeside	John walks towards Ann
17	2	MS	Lakeside	John talks to Ann

SCENE NO.	SHOT NO.	SHOT SIZE	LOCATION	DESCRIPTION

STORYBOARDING

SHOT NO. ________

SHOT NO. ________

SHOT NO. ________

SHOT NO. ________

SHOT NO. _____

SHOT NO. _____

SHOT NO. _____

SHOT NO. _____

SHOT NO. _____

SHOT NO. _____

SHOT NO. _____

SHOT NO. _____

SHOT NO. _____

SHOT NO. _____

SHOT NO. _____

SHOT NO. _____

SHOT NO. _____

SHOT NO. _____

SHOT NO. _____

SHOT NO. _____

1. Celtx script www.celtx.com
One of the best, most versatile, free script programmes, used by Hollywood professionals to write the movies you see in cinemas.

2. MapAPic mapapic.com
Invaluable filming logistics app that helps you collect data on locations and easily share it with collaborators.

3. Filmic Pro www.filmicpro.com
Retain manual control of focus, ISO, shutter speed and more with this app. Used by director Sean Baker to make Sundance hit, *Tangerine*.

4. Magic Hour www.magichourapp.net
If you're looking for that gorgeous, peach-hued sky, this handy app will tell you the best time to film as well as offering info on local light quality.

5. Cinescope www.cinescopeapp.com
For those wanting to think outside the box, *Fruitvale Station* cinematographer Rachel Morrison built an app that allows you to shoot in a customised aspect ratio.

6. Horizon www.horizon.camera
This app allows the user to shoot horizontal videos – whatever the orientation of your smartphone.

7. Free Music Archive www.freemusicarchive.org
A vital resource for the no-budget filmmaker, this site offers a wealth of public-domain music.

8. Audacity www.audacityteam.org
This free, open source, multi-platform audio software allows for intricate multi-track recording and editing.

9. The Frugal Filmmaker www.youtube.com/user/thefrugalfilmmaker
This YouTube channel offers top-line information for people making movies on a shoestring budget.

10. Shooting People www.shootingpeople.org
An online independent filmmakers network that should be the first port of call for anyone searching for like-minded creatives.

180-degree rule 57
2001: A Space Odyssey..........................21
45 Years 51

A

Altman, Robert 29, 62
ambient sound 91
Anderson, Paul Thomas........................67
Anderson, Wes.......................................29
Antonioni, Michelangelo 42
Apocalypse Now 99
The Artist 49
aspect ratio...40

B

Baker, Sean 8, 34
Battleship Potemkin........................... 103
Baumbach, Noah.............................37, 46
Berberian Sound Studio 89
black and white 46
Blade Runner 99
Bonnie and Clyde 40
The Blair Witch Project 68, 77
Blood Simple 78
Boogie Nights 67
Boyle, Danny 89
Brazil..99
Breathless 65, 103
Bresson, Robert......................................89
budget 23, 112

C

Carruth, Shane 37
Cassavetes, John 24, 37, 45
cinematographer 27

Citizen Kane...21
close-ups.......................................45, 123
Coen brothers...78
composition 42
continuity 82
Coppola, Francis Ford..............66, 86, 99
credits..107
crew 27
Cuarón, Alfonso 67
Cutaways 85

D

Days of Heaven..............................29, 74
dialogue 73, 86
dolly shot 65
Donnie Darko 99
Dr. Jekyll and Mr. Hyde.......................29

E

editing...95–103
Eisenstein, Sergei 103
equipment 34, 120
Eraserhead..49
establishing shot....................................51
The Evil Dead..37
The Exorcist.................................. 89, 96
Exposure 77

F

fade.. 102
Following 37
Ford, Henry 6
formats..107
Frances Ha 37, 46
Friedkin, Wiliam.............................. 89, 96

G

geography 58
Gilliam, Terry...99
Godard, Jean-Luc.............. 65, 67, 81, 103
The Godfather......................................66
golden hour 74
Goodfellas..52
Gravity... 67
Greengrass, Paul 68

H

Haigh, Andrew 51
handheld..68
The Hateful Eight.................................40
Hawks, Howard 42
Hazanavicius, Michel 49
High Noon... 103
Hitchcock, Alfred.........15, 21, 58, 62, 103
Hunger...52

I

I am Cuba.. 67
indoor shooting.....................................70

J

jump cut 101
Jurassic Park 58

K

Kalatozov, Mikhail...................................67
Kassovitz, Mathieu.................................49
Kelly, Richard...99
Kubrick, Stanley............................ 21, 101

L

La Haine...49
Lang, Fritz 89
Lean, David....................................40, 101
Leigh, Mike..30
Leone, Sergio 45
lighting 70, 73, 74
Linklater, Richard 54
location 30
long shot..123
low-light conditions............................... 77
Lynch, David..49

M

M...89
magic hour 74
make-up 27
Malick, Terrence 29, 74
Mamoulien, Rouben 29
A Man Escaped....................................89
Man With a Movie Camera 21
Mann, Michael 99
master shot.....................................52, 123
McQueen, Steve 52
Miami Vice 99
microphones 91
mise en scène.......................................42
movement.......................................60, 78
music 88, 104

N

Nolan, Christopher 37

O

outdoor shooting..................................73
Ozu, Yasujiro 85

P

permits..81
pillow shot 85
Primer..37
production designer 27
production manager..............................27
Psycho.. 103
Pulp Fiction 29

R

Raging Bull...49
Raimi, Sam 37
rehearsals 32
Renoir, Jean 21
The Royal Tenenbaums......................29
The Rules of the Game 21
Ryan's Daughter..................................40

S

Schindler's List 49
Scorsese, Martin 7, 46, 49, 52, 60
Scott, Ridley.................................. 30, 99
screenplay 18
script..18, 124
script superviser 82
Shadows 24, 37
shooting schedule 12, 116
shot size 122
sound.........................73, 86, 91, 96, 104
sound recordist.....................................27
soundtrack 104
Spielberg, Steven 6, 24, 49, 58

storyboard..............................15, 126–130
Strickland, Peter...................................89
Sundance Film Festival.........................8

T

Tangerine..8, 34
Tarantino, Quentin.....................16, 29, 40
Taxi Driver 60
Touch of Evil 67
Trainspotting.......................................89
truck shot...65
two-shot..54, 123

U

Uncle Boonmee Who Can Recall His Past Lives... 103

V

Vertigo.. 21, 62
Vertov, Dziga..21

W

A Wedding..29
Weekend 67
Weerasethakul, Apichatpong............. 103
Welles, Orson 21, 67
wipe 101

Z

Zinneman, Fred..................................... 103
zoom..62

p16. Quentin Tarantino, Interview in *Empire Magazine* (1994)

p18. Paul Schrader in *Writers in Hollywood 1915–1951* by Ian Hamilton (1990)

p23. Charlie Chaplin, *My Autobiography* (1964)

p24. Orson Welles in *The Movie Business* by Henry Jaglom (1992)

p30. Ridley Scott, interview in *Entertainment Weekly* (2012)

p32. Alexander Mackendrick in *On Film-making: An Introduction to the Craft of the Director*, Paul Cronin, editor (2006)

p34. James Cameron, video interview for *Academy of Achievement* (2009)

p40. See www.rogerdeakins.com

p42. Martin Scorsese, quoted in *The New Yorker* (2011)

p45. Clint Eastwood in *Something to Do With Death*, Christopher Frayling (2000)

p46. W.G. Sebald in *Searching for Sebald: Photography after W.G. Sebald*, Vance Bell and Lise Patt (2006)

p52. Woody Allen, interview on www.rogeregbert.com (2014)

p58. Alfred Hitchcock in *Alfred Hitchcock Interviews*, Sidney Gottlieb (2003)

p101. Stanley Kubrick, quoted in *The Cinematic Theater*, Babak A. Ebrahimian (2004)

ACKNOWLEDGEMENTS

The author

This book would not have been possible without the trust and patience of Little White Lies' editor-in-chief, David Jenkins, as committed and encouraging a boss and torchbearer as one could ever hope to work for. Massive shout out to Studio MUTI, whose illustrative wizardry knows no bounds; and to Timba Smits for his incredible design and layout skills; and to the team at Laurence King Publishing for giving me the opportunity to write this book in the first place. To every filmmaker mentioned in these pages, and to those about to shoot their first frame of film, you have my respect and gratitude.

Little White Lies

LWLies would like to thank our Fantastic Four design team, Timba, Laurène, Oliver, Simon and the wizards down at Studio MUTI (Brad, Clint and Miné) for their (always) incredible illustrations. And many thanks to Marc, Gaynor, Sophie and Angus at Laurence King Publishing for all their assistance and advice. For brilliant research and sanity-checking, we'd also like to thank Dan Einav, Lena Hanafy, Ewan Cameron, Lauren Thompson and Rebecca Speare-Cole. Shout out to all the TCO London crew, particularly to Adam and Clive for keeping the boat steady. And, of course, to Matt for mainlining his deep passion for film into this project.